SCOTTISH
Wit & Humour

CAMILLA ZAJAC

BRADWELL
BOOKS

Published by Bradwell Books
9 Orgreave Close Sheffield S13 9NP
Email: books@bradwellbooks.co.uk

Complied by Camilla Zajac

British Library Cataloguing in Publication Data: a catalogue record for this
book is available
from the British Library.

1st Edition
ISBN: 9781902674582

Print: Gomer Press, Llandysul, Ceredigion SA44 4JL
Design by: JenksDesign
Illustrations: ©Tim O'Brien 2013

Jock finds himself in dire trouble. He's already lost his business and is having yet more serious financial problems. He's so desperate that he decides to ask God for help. 'God, please help me. Ah've lost ma wee store and if Ah dinna get some money, Ah'm going to lose my hoose too. Please let me win the lottery!'

Lottery night comes and goes! Someone else wins. Jock prays again. 'God, please let me win the lottery! Ah've lost my wee store, ma hoose and Ah'm going to lose ma car as weel!'

Lottery night comes and goes again! Still no luck... Jock prays again.

'Ah've lost ma business, ma hoose and ma car. Ma bairns are starving. Ah dinna often ask Ye for help and Ah have always been a good servant to Ye. PLEASE just let me win the lottery this one time so Ah can get back on ma feet!'

Suddenly there is a blinding flash as the heavens open and the voice of God Himself thunders:

'Jock at least meet Me half way and buy a ticket!'

Ewan decided to call his father-in-law 'The Exorcist' because every time he came to visit he made the spirits disappear.

Harry proudly drove his new convertible into town and parked it on the main street, he was on his way to the recycle centre to get rid of an unwanted gift, a foot spa, which he left on the back seat.

He had walked half way down the street when he realised that he had left the top down... with the foot spa in the back.

He ran all the way back to his car, but it was too late...

Another five foot spas had been dumped in the car.

A farmer's wife, who was rather stingy with her whisky, was giving her shepherd a drink. As she handed him his glass, she said it was extra good whisky, being fourteen years old. 'Weel, mistress,' said the shepherd regarding his glass sorrowfully, 'It's very small for its age.'

I never was, am always to be.

No one ever saw me, nor ever will.

And yet I am the confidence of all

To live and breathe on this terrestrial ball.

What am I?

Tomorrow.

What did the cheese salesman say?

'That cheese may be Gouda, but this one is Feta!'

Did you hear about the two men from the monastery who opened up a seafood restaurant? One was the fish friar, and the other was the chip monk.

I went into the woods and got it. I sat down to seek it. I brought it home with me because I couldn't find it. What is it?

A splinter

At an auction in Glasgow, a wealthy American announced that he had lost his wallet containing £10,000 and would give a reward of £100 to the person who found it.

From the back of the hall, a Scottish voice shouted, 'I'll give £150!'

Jock's nephew came to him with a problem. 'I have my choice of two women,' he said, 'A beautiful, penniless young girl whom I love dearly, and a rich old widow whom I can't stand.'

'Follow your heart; marry the girl you love,' Jock counselled.

'Very well, Uncle Jock,' said the nephew, 'That's sound advice.'

'By the way,' asked Jock 'Where does the widow live?'

Did you hear that they've crossed a Newfoundland and a Basset Hound? The new breed is a Newfound Asset Hound, a dog for financial advisors.

How many surrealists does it take to screw in a lightbulb?

Banana.

What goes around the world but stays in a corner?

A stamp.

Angus called in to see his friend Donald to find he was stripping the wallpaper from the walls. Rather obviously, he remarked 'You're decorating, I see.' to which Donald replied 'Naw.' I'm moving house.'

A man walks into a bookshop and says 'I hope you don't have a book on reverse psychology.'

When one does not know what it is, then it is something; but when one knows what it is, then it is nothing?

A riddle.

SCOTTISH Wit & Humour

All about, but cannot be seen.
Can be captured, cannot be held.
No throat, but can be heard.
What is it?

The wind.

I'm part of the bird that's not in the sky. I can swim in the ocean
and yet remain dry. What am I?

A shadow.

What does one star say to another star when they meet?

Glad to meteor!

An Englishman, an Irishman and a Scotsman walk into a bar.

The Barman says 'Is this a joke?'

I have holes in my top and bottom, my left and right and in the middle. What am I?

A sponge.

A Scotsman walking through a field, sees a man drinking water from a pool with his hand.

The Scotsman man shouts ' Awa ye feel hoor that's full Oâ coos Sharn'

(Don't drink the water, it's full of cow dung.)

The man shouts back 'I'm English! Speak English, I don't understand you'.

The Scotsman man shouts back 'Use both hands, you'll get more in.'

What gets wetter and wetter the more it dries?

A Towel.

A Scots boy came home from school and told his mother he had been given a part in the school play. 'Wonderful,' says the mother, 'What part is it?' The boy says 'I play the part of the Scottish husband!' The mother scowls and says: 'Go back and tell your teacher you want a speaking part.'

What gear were you in at the moment of the impact?

Gucci sweats and Reeboks.

He who has it doesn't tell it. He who takes it doesn't know it. He who knows it doesn't want it. What is it?

Counterfeit money.

Jock's wife Maggie went to the doctor complaining of pains in the stomach. The doctor told her it was 'just wind'. 'Just wind?' she screamed at him. 'It was just wind that blew down the Tay Bridge!'

What can you catch but not throw?

A cold.

What comes once in a minute, twice in a moment, but never in a thousand years?

The letter M.

One day Jock bought a bottle of fine whiskey and while walking home he fell.

Getting up, he felt something wet on his trousers.

He looked up at the sky and said, 'Oh lord, please I beg you let it be blood!'.

From the beginning of eternity

To the end of time and space

To the beginning of every end

And the end of every place.

What am I?

The letter 'e'.

A group of chess enthusiasts checked into a hotel and were standing in reception discussing their recent tournament victories. After about an hour, the manager came out of the office and asked them to move. 'But why?' they asked, as they walked off. 'Because,' he said 'I can't stand chess nuts boasting in an open foyer.'

Though it is not an ox, it has horns; though it is not an ass, it has a pack-saddle; and wherever it goes it leaves silver behind. What is it?

A snail.

A very popular Scotsman dies in Glasgow and his old widow wishes to tell all his friends at once so she goes to the newspaper and says

'I'd like tae place an obituary fur ma late husband' The man at the desk says 'OK, how much money dae ye have?'

The old woman replies '£5' to which the man says 'You won't get many words for that, but write something and we'll see if it's OK'. The woman writes something and hands it over the counter and the man reads 'Peter Reid, fae Parkheid, deid'.

He feels guilty at the shortness of the statement and encourages the old woman to write a few more things. The old woman ponders and then adds some more words and hand the paper over the counter again. The man then reads 'Peter Reid, fae Parkheid deid. Ford Mondeo for sale'.

What goes round the house and in the house but never touches the house?

The sun.

What walks all day on its head?

A nail in a horse shoe.

The more you take, the more you leave behind. What are they?

Footsteps.

Sam works in an office in Glasgow, he went into his boss's office. He said to him

'I'll be honest with you, I know the economy isn't great, but I have three companies after me, and I would like to respectfully ask for a pay rise.'

After a few minutes of haggling his manager finally agrees to a 5% raise, and Sam happily gets up to leave.

'By the way', asks the boss as Sam is getting up, 'Which three companies are after you?'

'The electric company, the water company, and the phone company', Sam replies.

Where do generals keep their armies?

Up their sleevies.

What is the longest word in the English language?

Smiles. Because there is a mile between its first and last letters.

What do you do if you are driving your car in Glasgow and you see a spaceman?

Park in it, of course.

A man enters a dark cabin. He has just one match with him. There is an oil lamp, a wood stove, and a fireplace in the cabin. What would he light first?

The match.

Ten Scottish Proverbs

1) No matter how much you applaud a jukebox, you have to put another quid in for an encore.

2) A little bit of disagreement keeps the talk long.

   Too much agreement kills a conversation.

3) He who marries a chicken soon gets henpecked.

4) Man proposes, God disposes.

5) Better be the lucky man than the lucky man's son.

6) Hang a thief when he's young, an he'll no steal when he's auld.

7) Him that's born to be hanged will never be drowned.

8) She spends money like a woman with no hands.

9) Like the wife's tongue, often better meant than timed.

10) Marriages are all happy. It's having breakfast together that causes most of the trouble.

What is it that never asks you any questions and yet you answer?

Your phone.

Your mother's brother's only brother-in-law is your Stepfather, Grandfather, Uncle or Father?

Your Father.

Six dozen dozen is greater than half a dozen dozen   yes or no?

No, both are equal.

Two boys were arguing when the teacher entered the room.

The teacher says, 'Why are you arguing?'

One boy answers, 'We found a ten pound note and decided to give it to whoever tells the biggest lie.

'You should be ashamed of yourselves,' said the teacher, 'When I was your age I didn't even know what a lie was.'

The boys gave the ten pound note to the teacher.

The First Minister is being shown around a hospital. Towards the end of the visit, he is shown into a ward with a number people with no obvious signs of injury or disease.

He goes to greet the first patient and the man replies:

'Fair fa' your honest sonsie face, Great chieftain e' the puddin' race! Aboon them a' ye tak your place, Painch, tripe, or thairm; Weel are ye wordy o' a grace as lang's my arm.'

The FM is somewhat confused but goes to the next patient and greets him. The patient replies:

'Some hae meat, and canna eat, and some wad eat that want it, but we hae meat and can eat, and sae the Lord be thankit.'

The third starts rattling off as follows:

'Wee sleekit, cow'rin, tim'rous beastie, O, what a panic's in thy breastie! Thou need na start awa sae hasty, wi bickering brattle! I wad be laith to rin an chase thee, wi murdering pattle!'

The First Minister turns to the doctor accompanying him and asks what sort of ward is this - a mental ward?

'No,' replies the doctor, 'It's the Burns unit.'

A duck walks into a pub and goes up to the barman.

The barman says 'What can I get you?'

Duck: 'Umm. Do you have any grapes?'

Barman (Looking surprised):

'No, I'm afraid we don't.'

The duck waddles slowly out of the pub.

The next day at the same time, the duck waddles into the pub, hops up on a bar stool.

Barman: 'Hi. What can I get for you?'

Duck: 'Um. Do you have any grapes?'

Barman (a little annoyed): 'Hey! Weren't you in here yesterday. Look mate, we don't have any grapes. OK?'

The duck hops off the stool and waddles out of the door.

The next day, at the same time, the barman is cleaning some glasses when he hears a familiar voice

Duck: 'Umm... Do you have any grapes?'

The barman is really annoyed

Barman: 'Look. What's your problem? You came in here yesterday asking for grapes, I told you, we don't have any grapes! Next time I see your little ducktail waddle in here I'm going to nail those little webbed feet of yours to the floor. GOT me pal?'

So the duck hops off the bar stool and waddles out.

The next day at the same time, the duck waddles into the pub, walks up to the barman and the barman says,

'What on earth do YOU want?'

'Errrr. do you have any nails?'

'What!? Of course not.'

'Oh. Well, do you have any grapes?'

My life can be measured in hours;

I serve by being devoured.

Thin, I am quick; fat, I am slow.

Wind is my foe.

What am I?

A candle.

What kind of coat can only be put on when wet?

A coat of paint.

A man wanted to become a monk so he went to the monastery and talked to the head monk.

The head monk said, 'You must take a vow of silence and can only say two words every three years.'

The man agreed and after the first three years, the head monk came to him and said, 'What are your two words?'

'Food cold!' the man replied.

Three more years went by and the head monk came to him and said 'What are your two words?'

'Robe dirty!' the man exclaimed.

Three more years went by and the head monk came to him and said, 'What are your two words?'

'I quit!' said the man.

'Well', the head monk replied, 'I'm not surprised. You've done nothing but complain ever since you got here!'

My thunder comes before the lightning:

My lightning comes before the clouds:

My rain dries all the land it touches.

What am I?

A volcano.

Four men sat down to play,

and played all night till break of day.

They played for gold and not for fun,

with separate scores for every one.

Yet when they came to square accounts,

they all had made quite fair amounts!

Can you the paradox explain?

If no one lost, how could all gain?

The four men were all fiddlers in a band and were each paid £5 at the
end of the night. It is tempting to assume that they were playing cards,
but that is not stated!

Filming in Scotland can be difficult due to the ever-changing weather.

A film crew were filming in the highlands when an old Gaelic seer came hobbling by

'Tomorrow rain.' he informed them and hobbled on

Sure enough it rained the very next day. Again he hobbled past.

'Tomorrow sunshine.' he said, and it was indeed a fine sunny day the next day.

The director was very impressed and got the crew to hire him and every day the wise old sage predicted accurately what the weather would be.

But after a couple of weeks the old man didn't show up and eventually the director found him in a field.

'Hey, we need your predictions, why aren't you showing up?'

'Radio broken.' the old man replied.

A new client had just come in to see a famous lawyer.

'Can you tell me how much you charge?', said the client.

'Of course', the lawyer replied, 'I charge £200 to answer three questions!'

'Well that's a bit steep, isn't it?'

'Yes it is,' said the lawyer, 'And what's your third question?'

What, when you need it you throw it away, but when you don't need it you take it back?

An anchor.

A customer ordered some coffee in a café. The waitress arrived with the coffee and placed it on the table. After a few moments, the customer called for the waitress 'Waitress,' he said, 'There's dirt in my coffee!', 'That's not surprising, sir', replied the waitress, 'It was ground only half an hour ago.'

I am seen in places that appear to need me not.

I come seldom to places that need me most.

Sometimes my arrival is celebrated.

at others times I am hated.

I refresh all things whether they need it or not.

Rain.

A Lewis man was planning a flight to Glasgow and phoned to find out how long the flight would be. 'Just one second, sir' said the woman at the other end.

'Thanks very much' he replied and hung up.

Language student to teacher, 'Are 'trousers' singular or plural?'

Teacher, 'They're singular on top and plural on the bottom.'

Jock was travelling by train seated next to a stern-faced clergyman. As Jock pulled out a bottle of whisky from his pocket the clergyman glared and said reprovingly, 'Look here, I am sixty-five and I have never tasted whisky in my life!'

'Dinna worry, Minister,' smiled Jock, pouring himself a dram. 'There's no risk of you starting now!'

A passenger in a taxi tapped the driver on the shoulder to ask him something.

The driver screamed, lost control of the cab, nearly hit a bus, drove up

over the curb and stopped just inches from a large plate glass window.

For a few moments everything was silent in the cab, then the driver said, 'Please, don't ever do that again. You scared the daylights out of me.'

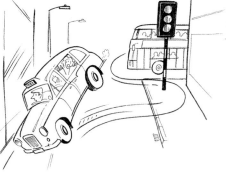

The passenger, who was also frightened, apologised and said he didn't

realize that a tap on the shoulder could frighten him so much, to which the driver replied, 'I'm sorry, it's really not your fault at all. Today is my

first day driving a cab. I've been driving a hearse for the last 25 years.'

What do you call six weeks of rain in Scotland?

Summer!

You can have me but cannot hold me:
Gain me and quickly lose me.
If treated with care I can be great.
And if betrayed I will break.
What am I?

Trust.

What kind of ears does an engine have?

Engineers.

What lies at the bottom of the ocean and twitches?

A nervous wreck.

What jumps when it walks and sits when it stands?

A kangaroo.

How do you get a Highlander onto the roof?

Tell him the drinks are on the house.

Why was the computer so tired when it got home?

Because it had a hard drive!

I give you a group of three. One is sitting down and will never get up. The second eats as much as is given to him, yet is always hungry. The third goes away and never returns. What are they?

A stove, fire and smoke.

Little Jock was in the garden filling in a hole when his English neighbour peered over the fence. Interested in what the mad man was up to, he politely asked, 'What are you doing there, Jock?' 'My goldfish died,' replied Jock tearfully without looking up, 'I've just buried him.' The English neighbour was very concerned. 'That's an awfully big hole for a goldfish, isn't it?' Jock patted down the last heap of dirt then replied, 'That's because he's inside your cat.'

Did you hear about the Scotsman who washed his kilt?

He couldn't do a fling with it.

I am so small, and sometimes I'm missed.

I get misplaced, misused, and help you when you list.

People usually pause when they see me,

So can you tell me what I could be?

A comma.

Hamish was building a garden shed and he ran out of nails so he went to the hardware store to buy some more. 'How long do you want them?' asked the shopkeeper. 'Oh, I need to keep them,' replied Hamish.

Light as a feather,

Nothing in it.

Few can hold it.

For even a minute.

Your breath.

What do you get when you cross a dog with a telephone?

A Golden Receiver!

What do cats like to eat for breakfast?

Mice Krispies

What always ends everything?

The letter 'g'.

Why do bagpipers walk when they play?

They're trying to get away from the noise.

Did you hear about the man who was convicted of stealing luggage from the airport?

He asked for twenty other cases to be taken into account.

Two aerials meet on a roof - fall in love - get married. The ceremony was rubbish - but the reception was brilliant.

McDougal bought two tickets for the lottery. He won five million pounds. 'How do you feel about your big win?' asked a newspaper reporter. 'Disappointed,' said McDougal, 'My other ticket didn't win anything.'

They say an Englishman laughs three times at a joke. The first time when everybody gets it, the second a week later when he thinks he gets it, the third time a month later when somebody explains it to him.

An Australian entered a bar and stood beside a Scotsman. 'Where are you from, pal?' asked the Scotsman, after they'd chatted for a while. 'I'm from the finest country in the whole wide world,' said the Australian. 'Are you?' said the other. 'You have a damn funny accent for a Scotsman.'

When I am filled,

I can point the way;

When I am empty,

Nothing moves me.

I have two skins,

One without and one within.

What am I?

A glove.

Old Jock was dying. Tenderly, his wife knelt by his bedside and asked: 'Anything I can get you, Jock?' No reply. 'Have you got a last wish, Jock?' Faintly, came the answer. . . 'A wee bit of that boiled ham over yonder.' 'Wheesht, man,' said his wife, 'you know fine that's for your funeral.'

A man went on a trip on Friday, stayed for two days and returned on Friday. How is that possible?

Friday is a horse!

An Englishman went into a hardware store and asked to buy a sink.

'Would you like one with a plug?' asked the assistant.

'Don't tell me they've gone electric,' said the Englishman.

When is a yellow dog most likely to enter a house?

When the door is open.

MacDonald was in poor health. He asked his friend MacDougal if he would pour a bottle of scotch over his grave if he should die one of these days. MacDougal said, 'Sure'n I'll be glad, laddie, but would you mind if I passed it through my kidneys first?'

I do not breathe, but I run and jump.

I do not eat, but I swim and stretch.

I do not drink, but I sleep and stand.

I do not think, but I grow and play.

I do not see, but you see me every day.

I am a leg

Why couldn't Cinderella be a good soccer player?

She lost her shoe, she ran away from the ball, and her coach was a pumpkin.

What do you call a boomerang that won't come back?

A stick.

What has a head like a cat, feet like a cat, a tail like a cat, but isn't a cat?

A kitten.

What did Geronimo shout when he jumped out of the aeroplane?

ME!

If vegetarians eat vegetables, what do humanitarians eat?

What do you call a hippie's wife?

Mississippi.

What was given to you, belongs to you exclusively and yet is used more by your friends than by yourself?

Your name.

Why is a Scottish boy with a cold like a soldier with seven days' leave?

Because they both have a wee cough (week off).

If it's not the day after Monday or the day before Thursday, and it isn't Sunday tomorrow, and it wasn't Sunday yesterday, and the day after tomorrow isn't Saturday, and the day before yesterday wasn't Wednesday, what day is it?

Sunday.

A life-long city man, tired of the rat race in his home town of Edinburgh, decided he was going to give up the city life, move to the country, and become a chicken farmer. He bought a nice organic chicken farm in the in Fife and moved in. It turned out that his next door neighbour was also a chicken farmer. A neighbour came for a visit one day and said, 'Chicken farming isn't easy. So, to help you get started, I'll give you 100 chickens.'

The new chicken farmer was delighted. Two weeks later the neighbour dropped by to see how things were going. The new farmer said, 'Not too well mate. All 100 chickens died.' The neighbour said, 'Oh, I can't believe that. I've never had any trouble with my chickens. I'll give you 100 more.' Another two weeks went by and the neighbour dropped in again. The new farmer said, 'You're not going to believe this, but the second 100 chickens died too.' Astounded, the neighbour asked, 'What went wrong?'

The new farmer said, 'Well, I'm not sure whether I'm planting them too deep or too close together.'

The leader of a large vegetarian society just couldn't control himself any more. He just needed to try some pork, just to see what it tasted like. So one summer day he told his members he was going away for a break. He left town and headed to the nearest restaurant. After sitting down, he ordered a roasted pig, and impatiently waited for his delicacy. After just a few minutes, he heard someone call his name, and to his horror he saw one of his fellow members walking towards him. Just at that same moment, the waiter walked over, with a huge platter, holding a full roasted pig with an apple in its mouth. 'Isn't that something,' says the man after only a moment's pause, 'All I do is order an apple, and look what it comes with!'

A man is rushing to a hospital from a business trip because his wife has just gone into labour with twins, and there is a family tradition that the first family member to arrive gets to name the children. The man is afraid his wayward brother will show up first and give his kids horrible names. When he finally arrives at the hospital in a cold sweat he sees his brother sitting in the waiting room, waving, with a silly grin on his face. He walks unhappily in to see his wife who is scowling and holding two little babies, a boy and a girl. Almost afraid to hear it, the man asks, 'What did he name the girl?' 'Denise' says the wife. 'Hey that's not too bad! What did he name the boy?' 'De-nephew.'

Did you hear about the Scot who gave up golf?

He lost his ball.

Did you hear about the Scot who took up golf?

He found it.

A girl who was just learning to drive went down a one-way street in the wrong direction, but didn't break the law. How come?

She was walking.

A man walks into a doctor's office with two onions under his arms, a potato in his ear and a carrot up his nose. He asks the doctor: 'What's wrong with me?'

The doctor replies: 'You're not eating properly.'

What time does Sean Connery arrive at Wimbledon?

Tennish.

What do you get if you cross a nun and a chicken?

A pecking order!

A Scotsman, an Irishman, and an Englishman had dinner together. When the waiter came with the bill, the Scotsman promptly said he would take it. The next day the newspaper carried a headline: 'English Ventriloquist Murdered in Restaurant.'

A man builds a house rectangular in shape. All the sides have southern exposure. A big bear walks by. What colour is the bear? Why?

The bear is white because the house is built on the North Pole.

What's green and runs around the garden?

A hedge.

How do you know if you're a pirate or not?.

You just know you arrrrrhh.

What starts with a ·P·, ends with an ·E· and has thousands of letters?

The Post Office!

The old king is dying, and wants to leave his kingdom to the wiser of his two sons. He tells them that he will hold a horse-race, and the son whose horse is the last to reach the bridge and come back will inherit the realm. Immediately the younger son jumps on a horse and makes for the bridge at top speed. The king now knows that this is the wiser son, and leaves him the kingdom. Why?

The younger son jumped on the older son's horse. He realized that if they rode their own horses the race would never end.

A Scot is emigrating to Australia. Upon entry he is being interviewed by the immigration officer. When the officer asks the question, 'Do you have a criminal record?' the Scot replies, 'Well no . . . I didn't realise you still needed one to get in!'

A Scotsman was on a fishing trip in the woods of Canada. "What's that over yonder?' the Scotsman asked of his guide. 'That's a moose, eh,' said the guide. 'Aye!' exclaimed the Scotsman, with a raised eyebrow. 'If that be a moose, I'd hate to see your rats!'

How do you make a sausage roll?

Push it!

A Scot from Aberdeen was on holiday in London and every night he returned to his hotel full of the wonders of the city. His excitement caused another guest to ask: 'Is this your first visit?' 'Aye, it is.' 'You seem to be having a great time.' 'Aye, I am that.' 'Good.' 'And what's more, it's not just a holiday. It's my honeymoon as well.' 'Oh. Then where's your wife?' 'Och. She's been here before.'

Did you hear about the skeleton that wore a kilt?

It was Boney Prince Charlie.

Seen on a poster in Argyll:

DRINK IS YOUR ENEMY.

Adjacent to this was another poster which said:

LOVE YOUR ENEMY.

What's green and runs around the garden?

A hedge.

Did you hear about the last wish of the henpecked husband of a houseproud Edinburgh wife?

He asked to have his ashes scattered on the carpet.

Two snowmen are standing in a field. One says to the other 'That's funny, I can smell carrots.'

Why do seagulls live by the sea?

Because if they lived by the bay they would be called bagels.

Why was the scarecrow promoted?

He was outstanding in his field!

A dog ran into a butcher shop in Dundee and grabbed some sirloin steak off the counter. But the butcher recognized the dog as belonging to a neighbour of his who happened to be a lawyer. The butcher called up his neighbour and said, 'If your dog stole steak from my butcher shop, would you be liable for the cost of the meat?' The lawyer replied, 'Of course, how much was the sirloin?'

The butcher replied 'Seven pounds.' A few days later the butcher received a cheque for seven pounds - and an invoice that read 'Legal Consultation Service: £150.'

Unusual Scottish place names:

Achadhluachrach	Lost
Anstruther	Milngavie
Auhenshuggle	Odness
Auchtermuchty	Slackend
Backside	Tongue of Gangsta
Buttock Point	Turdees
Dull	Yondertown of Knock
Ecclefechan	
Grimness	
Kilconquhar	

The local train stopped at a station long enough for the passengers to stretch their legs.

Sniffing the fresh air with appreciation, a passenger said to the guard: 'Invigorating, isn't it?'

'No,' he replied. 'Inverurie.'

A Scotsman complained to a magazine that if they didn't stop printing Scottish jokes, he wouldn't borrow their magazine to read any more.

Notice seen in a field in the north of Scotland: *The farmer allows walkers to cross the field for free, but the bull charges.*

What type of cheese is made backwards?

Edam.

A high-rise building was going up in central Glasgow, and three steel erectors sat on a girder having their lunch. 'Oh, no, not cream cheese and walnut again', said the first, who came from Coatbridge. 'If I get the same again tomorrow, I'll jump off the girder.'

The second, who came from Airdrie, opened his packet. 'Oh, no, not a Caesar salad with salami and lettuce on rye,' he said. 'If I get the same again tomorrow, I'll jump off too.'

The third man, who came from Dufftown, opened his lunch. 'Oh, no, not another potato sandwich,' he said. 'If I get the same again tomorrow, I'll follow you two off the girder.'

The next day, the Coatbridge man got cream cheese and walnut. Without delay, he jumped. The Airdrie man saw he had Caesar salad with salami and lettuce on rye. With a wild cry, he leapt too. The Dufftown man then opened his lunchbox. 'Oh, no,' he said. 'Potato sandwiches.' And he too jumped.

The foreman, who had overheard their conversation, reported what had happened, and the funerals were held together.

'If only I'd known,' sobbed the wife of the Coatbridge man. 'If only he'd said,' wailed the wife of the Airdrie man. 'I don't understand it at all,' said the wife of the Dufftown man. 'He always got his own sandwiches ready.'

The local train stopped at a station long enough for the passengers to stretch their legs.

Sniffing the fresh air with appreciation, a passenger said to the guard: 'Invigorating, isn't it?'

'No,' he replied. 'Inverurie.'

When Jock moved to London he constantly annoyed his English acquaintances by boasting about how great Scotland was.

Finally, in exasperation, one said, 'If Scotland's so wonderful, how come you didn't stay there?' 'Well,' explained Jock 'They're all so clever up there I had to come down here to have any chance of making it at all.'

What's brown and sticky?

A twig.

When Sandy came back from his first trip to London, everyone in the village was keen to find out how he had got on.

'Did you like it?'

'Oh, it was no' bad.'

'As good as that, was it?'

'Well, there was just the one thing wrong. The other guests in my hotel just would not go to their beds. They were in the corridor ouside my room shouting and banging on my door until three o'clock in the morning.'

'So what did you do, Sandy?'

'Och, I just kept on playing my bagpipes.'

An American was going for a job interview in the Scottish countryside and on the way home, he asked a local farmer for directions:

'Excuse me dude could you possibly tell me the quickest way to London?'

The farmer said: 'You driving or walking, lad?'

The American replied: 'Driving.'

The farmer nodded, saying:

'Yup, definitely the quickest way'

What's the difference between roast beef and pea soup?

Anyone can roast beef.

What five letter word can have its last four letters removed and still sound the same?

QUEUE - remove "UEUE", say Q. Q, yes and queue are pronounced the same.

What has five eyes, but cannot see?

The Mississippi River.

Maitre d': 'Are you here for a special occasion?'

MacDonald: 'Aye, we won the third prize in the annual Robert Burns Contest - a haggis dinner for two.'

Maitre d': 'What were the other prizes?'

MacDonald: 'The second prize was a single haggis dinner, and, if you won the first prize, you didn't have to eat the haggis.'

The old soldier was reminiscing to his grandchildren about his wartime experiences with the Gordon Highlanders. 'Yes, I fought in Africa, Italy and Germany. I fought with Montgomery, I fought with Wavell and I fought with Alexander'. His granddaughter looked up and said 'Couldn't you get on with anybody, Granddad?'

Wullie was having his appendix out and was driving the doctor mad with questions. 'Will Ah be able to play the bagpipes after ma operation?' he asked. 'Of course you will!' snapped the doctor. 'That's amazing!' marvelled Wullie. 'Ah couldna play them before!'

Who is the roundest knight at King Arthur's table?

Sir Cumfrence

Hector and Hamish were delighted that they had finished a jigsaw puzzle in record time and told Sandy that the hundred pieces had only taken them six months to fit together. Sandy was unimpressed and said that sounded a long time. 'Not at all' said Hamish, 'It said on the box three to five years.'